THIS IS YOUR INDIA

OM SRIVASTAVA

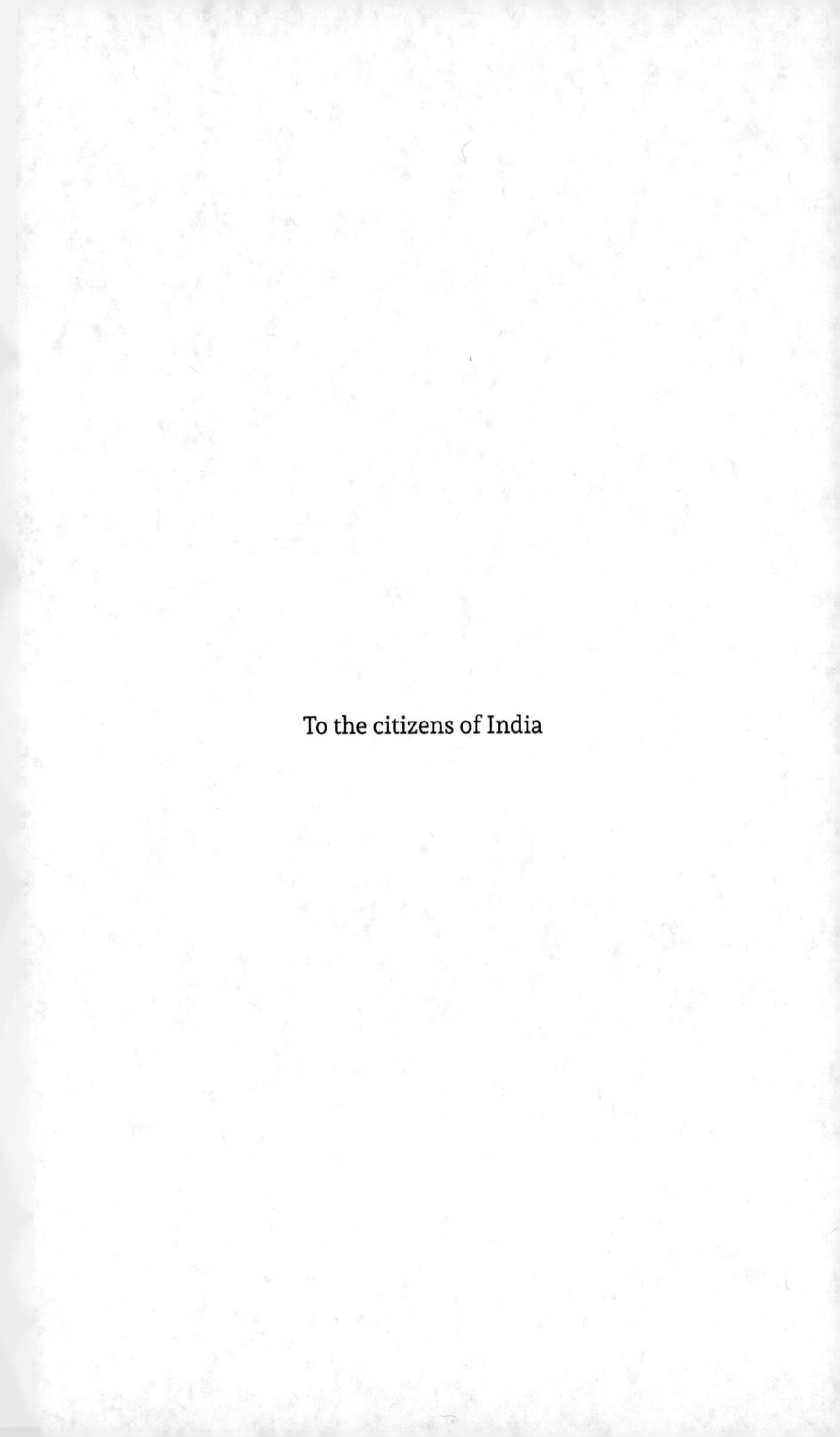

To the citizens of India

Contents

INDIA

AUTHOR

Om Srivastava

Acknowledgements

This is my first non-fiction book and it was really a tough job. I had to research a lot, but the stress level decreased as I started writing about my country. I would like to thank my family members for tremendous support. Amish sir's (AMISH TRIPATHI's) book Immortal India and respected Sadhguru's speeches helped me a lot. I also started believing in the universal head (GOD) while writing this book.

A SHORT NOTE FROM THE AUTHOR

Happy Reading........

PROLOGUE

Our India is an abode of knowledge. House of Gods. We have the answer to every question in our ancients scripts. Till today we have just found some scripts. And in that collection, just a few are translated. You must be thinking that why have I mentioned the scripts as some, even if we have discovered many scripts.

I have mentioned so, because some scripts say that India has a lot more ancient texts.

I
The Gods

There is just one leader who rules the world. But, in our Indian culture, we believe in that leader, by different names.

We call them: - Mahadev (Lord Shiva), Shri Ram (Lord Rama), Shri Krishna (Lord Krishna), Bhagwaan Vishnu (Lord Vishnu), Bramha Bhagwaan (Lord Brahma), Maa Durga (Goddess Durga), Maa Kali (Goddess Kali), Maa Parvati (Goddess Parvati) (there are many more in Hindu religion), Allah, Guru Nanak, Guru Gobind, Vardhamana Mahavir, Lord Buddha, Jesus, and many more.

In India, some preachers like Lord Buddha (Buddhism), Vardhamana Mahavir (Jainism), Guru Nanak (Sikhism) are thought to be God or an incarnation of God. They are also the founder of religions.

II

The Hindu Trinity

The Hindu Trinity – Brahma, Vishnu and Mahesh (Shiva)

<u>Did Brahma, Vishnu and Mahesh collectively create the world?</u>

There is a religious belief that:

Brahma, Vishnu and Mahesh collectively created the world. Brahma is the creator, Vishnu is the administrator, and Mahesh is the destroyer.

<u>So, what are the facts? Has the world really been created by these three Gods?</u>

The facts is that the names Brahma, Vishnu and Mahesh represent the three natural attributes of the *prakruti* (inherent qualities), which are present in every individual.

i. *pitt* (bilious component) in the body brings about *sattvik prakruti* (goodness, relative, awareness)

ii. *vayu* (airy component) which is responsible for *ajas prakruti* (passion, desires)

iii. *kaph* (phlegm component) that results in *tamas prakruti*

Every living being has prakruti and the prakruti is made up of inanimate matter. The intrinsic nature of inanimate matter is permanent, while the phases of prakrutiarise and die out every moment. The phases undergo constant creation and destruction.

Similarly, the soul is the eternal element in all living beings, whereas the phases of the soul undergo constant creation and destruction.

In a programme, the three identities namely Brahma, Vishnu and Mahesh were placed as symbolic representations to help people learn the functions of three attributes of a phase.

Brahma was placed at the point in which there is creation i.e. the phase arises. Vishnu was placed at the point where the phase remains steady or still. Lastly, Mahesh was placed at the point, where the destruction takes place.

This placement was very helpful and had good depth in it. However, the thing was created merely for the ease of the people's understanding; down the line, it was misinterpreted as the individuals who we believe as God or creator of the world were represented of symbols.

III

The ugly side of the human world

Everything in this world is not good for us.

Our human world has an ugly side too! There are worries, fears, miseries, tears, illness, pain, agony, and endless suffering across the world.

But...... this world is not created by God. This is created by us, the humans.

This is because we are not satisfied with what we have.

Lord Krishna said, "Once a person is satisfied with what he has, nothing can bring him suffering."

IV

Till yet

You must be thinking that why am I talking about God if I was supposed to talk about something related to India.

I am talking about these things because the knowledge about these arose from our ancient scripts.

V

Facts

- When many cultures were only nomadic forest dwellers over 5,000 years ago, Indians established Harappan culture in Sindhu Valley (Indus Valley Civilization).
- Chess was invented in India.
- Algebra and Trigonometry are studies, which originated in India.
- The 'Place Value System' and the 'Decimal System' were developed in India in 100 BC.
- The world's first granite temple is the Brihadeshwara Temple at Thanjavur, Tamil Nadu. The *shikhara* of the temple is made from a single 80-tonne piece of granite. This magnificent temple was built in just five years, (between 1004 AD and 1009 AD) during the reign of Rajaraja Chola.
- India is the largest democracy in the world, in the 7th largest country in the world, and one of the most ancient civilizations.

- The game of Snake & Ladders was created by the 13th century poet saint *Gyandev*. It was originally called *'Mokshapat'*. The ladders in the game represented virtues and the snakes indicated vices. The game was played with cowry shells and dices. In time, the game underwent several modifications, but its meaning remained the same, i.e. good deeds take people to heaven and evil to a cycle of re-births.

- The world's highest cricket ground is in Chail, Himachal Pradesh. Built in 1,893 after levelling a hilltop, this cricket pitch is 2,444 meters above sea level.

- India has the largest number of Post Offices in the world.

- The largest employer in India is the Indian Railways, employing over a million people.

- The University of Nalanda built in 4th century was one of the greatest achievements of ancient India in the field of education.

- Ayurveda is the earliest school of medicine known to mankind. The Father of Medicine, Acharya Charaka, consolidated Ayurveda 2,500 years ago.

- India was one of the richest countries till the time of British rule in the early 17th century. Christopher Columbus, attracted by India's wealth, had come looking for a sea route to India when he discovered America by mistake.

- The Art of Navigation & Navigating was born in the river Sindh over 6,000 years ago. The very word 'navigation' is derived from the Sanskrit word 'NAVGAITH'. The word 'navy' is also derived from a Sanskrit word 'NOU'.

- Bhaskaracharya rightly calculated the time taken by the earth to orbit the sun. According to his calculation, the time taken was 365.258756484 days.
- The value of 'pi' was calculated by the Indian Mathematician Budhyana, and he explained the concept of what is known as the Pythagorean Theorem. He discovered this in the 6th century, long before the European mathematicians.
- Quadratic Equations were used by Sridharacharya in the 11th century. The largest numbers the Greeks and the Roans used were 106 whereas Hindus used numbers as big as 10^{53} (10 to the power of 53) with specific names as early as 5000 BC during the Vedic period. Even today, the largest used number is 10^{12} (10 to the power of 12).
- Until 1896, India was the only source of diamond in the whole world.
- The Baily Bridge is the bridge at the highest elevation in the world. It is located in the Ladakh valley between the Dras and Suru rivers in the Himalayan Mountains. It was built by the Indian Army in August 1982.
- Sushruta is regarded as the Father of Surgery. Over 2,600 years ago, Sushruta and his team conducted complicated surgeries like cataract, artificial limbs, caesareans, fractures, removing urinary stones, plastic surgeries and brain surgeries.
- Usage of anaesthesia was well known in ancient Indian medicine. Detailed knowledge of anatomy embryology, digestion, metabolism, physiology, etiology, genetics and immunity is also found in many ancient Indian texts.
- The four religions born in India – Hinduism, Buddhism, Jainism, and Sikhism, are followed by 25%

of the world's population.

- There are 300,000 active mosques in India. It is more than in any other country, including the Muslim world.
- Jews and Christians have lived continuously in India since 200 BC and 52 AD respectively.
- The largest religious building in the world is Angkor Wat, a Hindu Temple in Cambodia built at the end of 11th century by the Indian Kings. It was started by Suryavarman II and completed by Jayavarman VII.
- Varanasi, also known as Banaras was called 'the ancient city' when Lord Buddha visited it in 500 BC; and is the oldest, continuously inhabited city in the world today.
- India provides safety for more than 300,000 refugees originally from Sri Lanka, Tibet, Bhutan and Bangladesh, who escaped to flee religious or political persecutions.
- Martial Arts were first created in India, and later spread to Asia by Buddhist missionaries.
- Yoga has its origin in India and has existed for over 5,000 years.

VI
Reviving India

Nowadays, we Indians are forgetting our culture. To bring it back we need to re-write the history. Not from the last 3,000 years or last 10,000 years; but, from the start.

India's history and culture is dynamic, spanning back to the beginning of human civilization.

We are forgetting the victories, the discoveries, the inventions of our country because of the education system across India. They tell us that we were looted, beaten, criticised by other people, but we are never told that we worth a lot to the whole world. Let me explain you why:

The Indian kings went and built Angkor Thom and Angkor Wat in Cambodia. Angkor Wat is the largest religious building on this planet. , If you go and see the intricacy, sheer design and engineering of how these temples are built, you will feel proud of being a human. Proud, because of human beings could think something like this, at thousand years ago, it's just too much.

Now, just tell. How many of you were taught this by your history teacher in school?

As I said earlier, we are only told that how we were conquered, looted, beaten, criticised by others. Now, if there is no pride, why would anyone like to re-create or develop our culture? We need to understand this. When humans attach their nation to their identity, they would do everything to make it safe and clean. But, why would anyone attach their nation to their identity, if there is no pride.

VII
The fault of citizens

As I wrote earlier, everything in this world is not good for us.

Our human world has an ugly side too! There are worries, fears, miseries, tears, illness, pain, agony, and endless suffering across the world, and they are created by the humans.

In the upcoming two chapters, I will tell you all, about the things that bring negativity.

VIII

Caste system

Caste system is something that has reduced a lot in India, but not completely disappeared. Some people still discriminate the ones of lower castes. If people look back in the ancient time period, they will come to know to that the great thinker and philosopher, Satyakama Jabala, was from a low caste.

IX

People's attitude towards the poor

The poor people in India face a lot of problem.

People go to temples and give a lot of donation. But they give a very less amount of money to the beggars. They can even give some food to poor.

The houses that are given to the poor, by the government are taken up by the corrupt public servants. The poor doesn't even complain, in the fear of the government employee.

If a poor is selling something, the people will start bargaining, but if they go to a mall or a supermarket, they will not bargain, as they feel that the thing is branded. The poor hawker gets manipulated by the costumer and falls in the trap of bargaining.

Saare Jahan Se Achcha

Saare Jahan Se Achcha Hindustaan Hamaara

www.ingramcontent.com/pod-product-compliance
Lightning Source LLC
Chambersburg PA
CBHW050757250726
48662CB00005B/2278